Akathist to Saint John of Tolbolsk

Kontakion 1

ɔsen miracle worker and wise shepherd, luminary of God, shining in the land of Siberia. We
ise you with love for your miracles. As You stand before the eternal glory of the King of
aven, intercede that all troubles may be kept from them who sing to You. Rejoice, holy Father
ɪn, wonder-worker of Siberia!

Ekos 1

ɪu have kindled the holy flame of faith in the Almighty God; you have loved these little ones,
ɔm God the Word calls His brethren; therefore you have amazed the angels with your glorious
ɔ. And we revere you, Holy Father, as we cry out:

oice, stone of the Orthodox faith;

oice, light of Christian love;

oice, servant of Christ's righteousness;

oice, bearer of God's truth;

oice, you glorify your Father in heaven through your good works;

oice, in the glory of God, who reigns with all the saints;

oice, with your love surrounding those who suffer;

oice, through your prayer you save those who perish;

oice, holy Father John, wonder-worker of Siberia!

Kontakion 2

Seeing the sea of life stirred up by the storm of adversity, to the calm refuge of the monastery o
Pechersk you drew near, O' cross-bearer, and renouncing the perishable world, you sang unto th
Eternal God: Alleluia!

Ekos 2

As a faithful servant, you have multiplied the talent of grace, through your work and toil; theref
the Lord calls you to eternal joy. And we sing unto you, O God-wise:

Rejoice, you have kept your mind pure;

Rejoice, through vigil and fasting you put to death the passions of the flesh;

Rejoice, you have overcome the evil one with humility;

Rejoice, you have obtained incorruptible riches;

Rejoice, you have a great heart of patience;

Rejoice, eagle, soaring to heaven in the mind;

Rejoice, stranger on the way of the cross;

Rejoice, heir to the kingdom of heaven;

Rejoice, holy Father John, wonder-worker of Siberia!

Kontakion 3

the power of the Cross you fearlessly struggled against the prince of this world, fighting for the urch and raising up the sign of Christ's victory with the song: Alleluia!

Ekos 3

th your abundant mercy for all men, you are a comfort to those who mourn, an admonition to se who go astray, an intercession for those who suffer, a tireless guardian for the weak and the dow, and a helper to all in salvation; we thank you God, who is wonderful in His saints, for om we bring this hymn to you:

joice, your will be done in harmony with God's will;

joice, you have known grace through faith;

joice, through faith you have received the grace of virtue;

joice, giving all yourself to the poor;

joice, constant in mercy;

joice, physician without remuneration;

joice, you who serve the infirm;

joice, you truly please Christ;

joice, holy Father John, wonder-worker of Siberia!

Kontakion 4

e evil one will stir up envy in the hearts of self-loving servants, and teach the proud to slander u before kings, so that your work may be destroyed by the champions of godliness; but God will ng out your truth as light, and will save you in humility when you sing to Christ: Alleluia!

Ekos 4

Hearing the lamentation of those in distress in the days of famine, You have called Your spiritu
children to share their daily bread, saving human souls from famine and eternal death; therefore
accept this singing in honour and glory:

Rejoice, full of the bread of heaven;

Rejoice, full of the drink of immortality;

Rejoice, a disciple of the God of the Word;

Rejoice, you who have been graced with the Holy Spirit;

Rejoice, full of the Father in heaven;

Rejoice, you who are in the temple of the Holy Trinity;

Rejoice, deliverance from trouble and sorrow;

Rejoice, you are the correction of the wicked heart;

Rejoice, holy Father John, wonder-worker of Siberia!

Kontakion 5

You have shone in the darkness of ignorance, by the rays of the Gospel, you have penetrated in
the hearts of men and encouraged all to sing to the Sun of Righteousness, Christ: Alleluia!

Ekos 5

ing the darkness of ignorance that covers men, you dispersed the riches of Christ's teaching

erously; working tirelessly, drawing strength in prayer from the source of wisdom. For this

on we honour your memory, crying out:

oice, adorned with the grey hair of wisdom;

oice, glorified by the virtue of humility;

oice, God-inspired teacher;

oice, patron of spiritual enlightenment;

oice, you clear-flowing stream of divine knowledge;

oice, preacher of the True Light.

oice, as you have taught the young;

oice, as you have opened the minds of babes;

oice, holy Father John, wonder-worker of Siberia!

Kontakion 6

acher of the glory of God in deed and in word, by whom you were chosen as your successor by

at Theodosius, with whom in the kingdom of heaven you sing: Alleluia!

Ekos 6

You shone in the house of God, luminary of Christ, John, when you were chosen by the faithful bishop, after the blessed death of Saint Theodosius. And faithfully delivered up his flock, singing

Rejoice, who clothed you with wisdom;

Rejoice, for your beauty adorns you with light;

Rejoice, clothed in the garment of salvation;

Rejoice, you humble minister;

Rejoice, crowned with glory;

Rejoice, chosen shepherd;

Rejoice, you preserve your sheep;

Rejoice, feast of love;

Rejoice, holy Father John, wonder-worker of Siberia!

Kontakion 7

Blessed John, though you have received heavenly glory, you have written books in which you tell the faithful to trust in God and to sing to Him in tribulation: Alleluia!

Ekos 7

nt Theodosius appeared to you in your sickness, and commanded you to celebrate the Liturgy.
aking from the bed of sickness and giving thanks to Christ, rejoicing in this we sing unto you:

oice, keeper of the sweetness of prayer;

oice, keeper of the joy of grace;

oice, in tribulation and sickness you call on the Heavenly Physician;

oice, you have received healing through your faith;

oice, blossom of fragrance, you have flowered into immortality;

oice, for by the highness of your life ungodliness is shamed;

oice, for you help those who call on you;

oice, for in dreams and visions you visit the faithful;

oice, holy Father John, wonder-worker of Siberia!

Kontakion 8

see a wondrous miracle in you, O' God-bearer John, for in your old age you came to Siberia full
trength to serve Christ; the message of the truth of Orthodoxy went out from you to China, and
new people of God were taught to sing: Alleluia!

Ekos 8

In the land of exile you preached all things that are God's, multiplying the flock of those who are saved; therefore the Church honours you with this singing:

Rejoice, you who turn from idols to Christ;

Rejoice, for through the icons of the Mother of God your spiritual children are blessed;

Rejoice, for you warm Siberia with grace;

Rejoice, for you have driven away the night of sorrow;

Rejoice, for you have compassion on all;

Rejoice, for through your rule of life you have edified all;

Rejoice, one who visits prisons;

Rejoice, you true servant of Christ;

Rejoice, holy Father John, wonder-worker of Siberia!

Kontakion 9

You gave all your heart for the fulfilment of the righteousness of the Gospel, whereby you did ma good works, during the short time of your ministry in Tobolsk, secretly doing good and visiting prisoners in the name of Jesus Christ, to whom you call to sing: Alleluia!

Ekos 9

man can do justice to your holiness, for God Himself has glorified you by the wondrous end of
ur life, you celebrated the liturgy and, serving the poor in your house, you withdrew to prayer and
s you went to the Lord, bowing before the icon of Our Lady; and we sing the original hymn to
u in compassion:

joice, you have fallen asleep before the icon of the Mother of God;

joice, alive in heaven;

joice, worshipping Christ with the apostles;

joice, crowned with martyrs;

joice, shining in the Synaxis of the Holy Fathers;

joice, in the holy family of saints;

joice, granting the icon of the Mother of God to Tobolsk as a blessing;

joice, as this miraculous icon is our protection;

joice, holy Father John, wonder-worker of Siberia!

Kontakion 10

ant salvation to our souls, Father John, that righteousness and peace may shine in the midst of
ur flock and in the great Church that we may sing to God: Alleluia!

Ekos 10

A pillar to the poor and orphans, a comfort to those in tribulation, a healing to those who are ill, a
illumination to those who are blind. For this reason, in adoration of your holiness, we sing to you

Rejoice, for your earthly work continues;

Rejoice, for you remain the guardian of our salvation;

Rejoice, you who fast and pray and cast out evil spirits;

Rejoice, who strengthens the weak;

Rejoice, luminary of God;

Rejoice, preacher of faith, healer of the deaf;

Rejoice, multitudes come to you for your holiness;

Rejoice, as from afar they pray to you for salvation;

Rejoice, holy Father John, wonder-worker of Siberia!

Kontakion 11

Take this song as a humble gift from us, Father John, and ask for the perfect gift of love, so that
may see the glory of God and hear in heaven: Alleluia!

Ekos 11

everend father, you are a shining sun, risen in the darkness of sin, for He who lives for ever gave

power to cast out demons and to gather the faithful in prayer, bequeath to the generation who

ʁe to honour you your paternal blessing:

ɔice, for you have dispelled the clouds of unbelief;

ɔice, for through faith you illumine dark souls;

ɔice, for you revive the hope of salvation;

ɔice, for you have saved those in despair;

ɔice, for you raise the fallen;

ɔice, for you have lifted up the despondent;

ɔice, for you have taken away every tear of the afflicted;

ɔice, for you are the one who brings forth the tears of repentance;

ɔice, holy Father John, wonder-worker of Siberia!

Kontakion 12

grace of healing flowed from your holy relics, and your children gathered together from all the

s of the Russian land to the place of your burial, to cry out to God: Alleluia!

Ekos 12

Singing to the merciful God with light in their souls and burning candles in their hands, the faith
brought your relics, and carried them around the Church of Sophia, and they saw with tears of
tenderness that heaven and earth would stand with us, reverently crying out:

Rejoice, companion of the angels;

Rejoice, servant of the Holy Church;

Rejoice, patron of your flock;

Rejoice, for before your marvellous icon of the Mother of God, interceding for us;

Rejoice, for you have seen the first image of the Mother of God;

Rejoice, as you stand before the Most Holy Trinity;

Rejoice, you offer the censer of propitiation for us before God;

Rejoice, intercessor of our salvation;

Rejoice, holy Father John, wonder-worker of Siberia!

Kontakion 13

Accept this prayer, and offering it to the throne of the Most High, ask that peace and faith be
established in our Orthodox country, that God's kingdom be established for the people, and that t
be justified before the eyes of the awesome Judge singing: Alleluia! (thrice)

Ekos 1

ı have kindled the holy flame of faith in the Almighty God; you have loved these little ones,
ɔm God the Word calls His brethren; therefore you have amazed the angels with your glorious
. And we revere you, Holy Father, as we cry out:

oice, stone of the Orthodox faith;
oice, light of Christian love;
oice, servant of Christ's righteousness;
oice, bearer of God's truth;
oice, you glorify your Father in heaven through your good works;
oice, in the glory of God, who reigns with all the saints;
oice, with your love surrounding those who suffer;
oice, through your prayer you save those who perish;
oice, holy Father John, wonder-worker of Siberia!

Kontakion 1

ɔsen miracle worker and wise shepherd, luminary of God, shining in the land of Siberia. We
ıse you with love for your miracles. As You stand before the eternal glory of the King of
ıven, intercede that all troubles may be kept from them who sing to You. Rejoice, holy Father
n, wonder-worker of Siberia!

Prayer to Saint John

O Good Shepherd, Father John, the righteous path of your life has led you to the eternal Sun of righteousness. You sought God with all your soul, loving Him more than life. But we are far from the goodness of God, walking after our own wicked will, loving vain pleasures, despising the salvation of our souls, shutting our hearts to hear the word of God, and turning away from brotherly love. Let us not be lost in the mud of our sins, but raise up for us a prayer to the Lord, that He may have mercy on us and grant us repentance; that the abyss of licentiousness, malice, and treason may not consume us; that the internal strife may fall silent; that our land may be spared the famine and the wrath of God; and that peace may reign among the earth. Hear us sinners, Holy Hierarch of God, reveal to us your wondrous intercession, visit us who are weak, poor, needy, and lost sheep of your flock: heal our infirmities, strengthen to patiently bear the cross of life, listen to the groaning of the suffering, and look to the tears of the weak and sorrowful. We are sick in soul and weary in heart; champion of the truth, pray that those who have fallen away may return to the bosom of the Church of Christ; that the name of God may be glorified in us; that righteousness and love may reign in our land; that we may be worthy to receive the peace of Christ our God; that joy in the Lord may shine in our hearts; and that we may bless the Most Pure and Majestic Name of the One True and Perfect Trinity, Father and Son and Holy Ghost, for ever and ever. Amen.

Troparion tone 8:

Educator of piety, nourisher of orphans, comforter of those in pain, physician of the afflicted, sweet helper of the soul to those who suffer, warm intercessor for all in the Lord, holy father of our Lord John, beseech Christ God to save our souls.

Kontakion tone 2:

Educator of those in the darkness of ignorance, comforter of widows and orphans, wondrous doctor of the weak, instructor of infants and adolescents, and a shining light to parents, holy father John beseech Christ God, to grant our country confirmation in faith, to our army victory over its enemies and great mercy to your people.

gnification:

magnify you, Father John, and commemorate your memory, for you have prayed for us through
rist our God.

Printed in Great Britain
by Amazon

21728733R00020